Mm

mop

M m

MILK

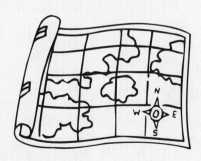

Name _____

Initial m Trace and write the letters. Color the pictures whose names begin with the *m* sound.

1

m m

2   **Initial m**   Trace and write the letters. Write *m* below each picture whose name begins with the *m* sound.

D d

dog

D d

Name _____

Initial d   Trace and write the letters. Color the pictures whose names begin with the *d* sound.

3

© 1991 Steck-Vaughn Company

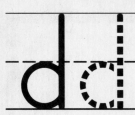

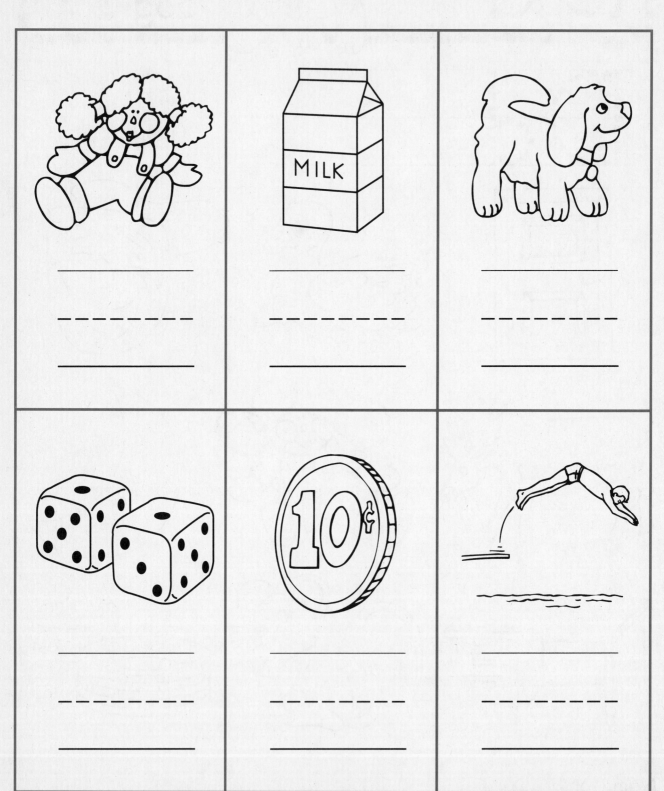

4   **Initial d**   Trace and write the letters. Write *d* below each picture whose name begins with the *d* sound.

F f

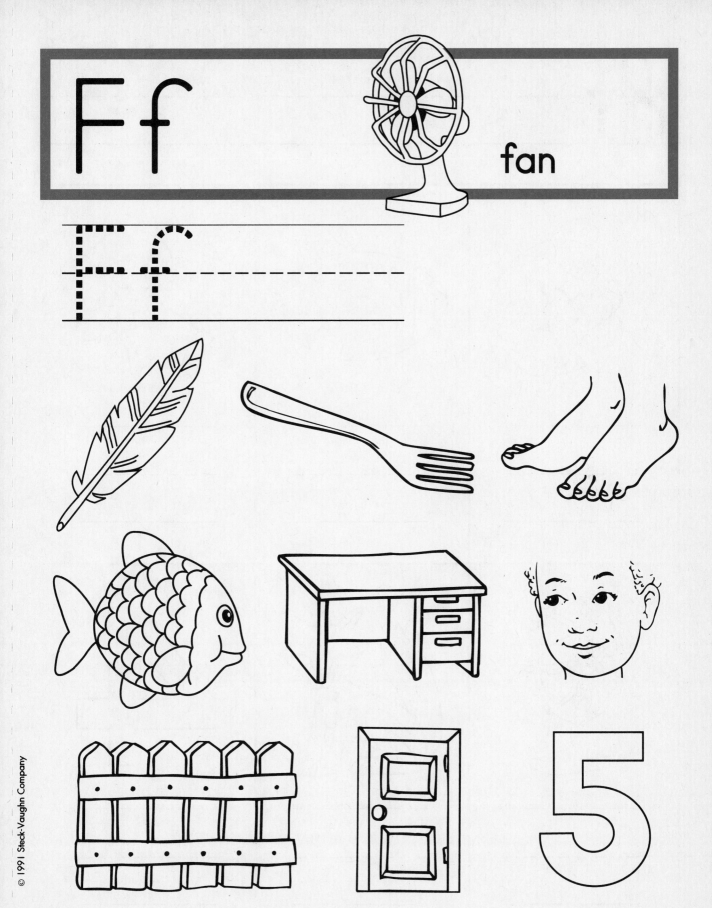

fan

F f

Name _____

Initial f   Trace and write the letters. Color the pictures whose names begin with the *f* sound.

5

Initial f Trace and write the letters. Write *f* below each picture whose name begins with the *f* sound.

m d f

_ _ _ _ _ _ _

_ _ _ _ _ _ _

_ _ _ _ _ _ _

_ _ _ _ _ _ _

_ _ _ _ _ _ _

_ _ _ _ _ _ _

_ _ _ _ _ _ _

_ _ _ _ _ _ _

_ _ _ _ _ _ _

MILK

_ _ _ _ _ _ _

_ _ _ _ _ _ _

5

_ _ _ _ _ _ _

_ _ _ _ _ _ _

Name _____

Reviewing Initial m, d, f   Write the letter that stands for the first sound in each picture name.

Reviewing Initial m, d, f Trace the paths from the boy to each pet. Then write the letter that stands for the first sound in each picture on each path.

m	m	m
d	d	d
f	f	f

m	m	m
d	d	d
f	f	f

m	m	m
d	d	d
f	f	f

Name _____

Final m, d, f Circle the letter that stands for the last sound in each picture name.

m d f

Final m, d, f Write the letter that stands for the last sound in each picture name.

G g

 goat

G g

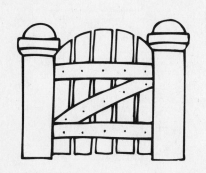  

Name _____

Initial g Trace and write the letters. Color the pictures whose names begin with the *g* sound.

11

g g

Initial g   Trace and write the letters. Write *g* below each picture whose name begins with the *g* sound.

B b

bus

B b

Name _____

Initial b   Trace and write the letters. Color the pictures whose names begin with the *b* sound.

13

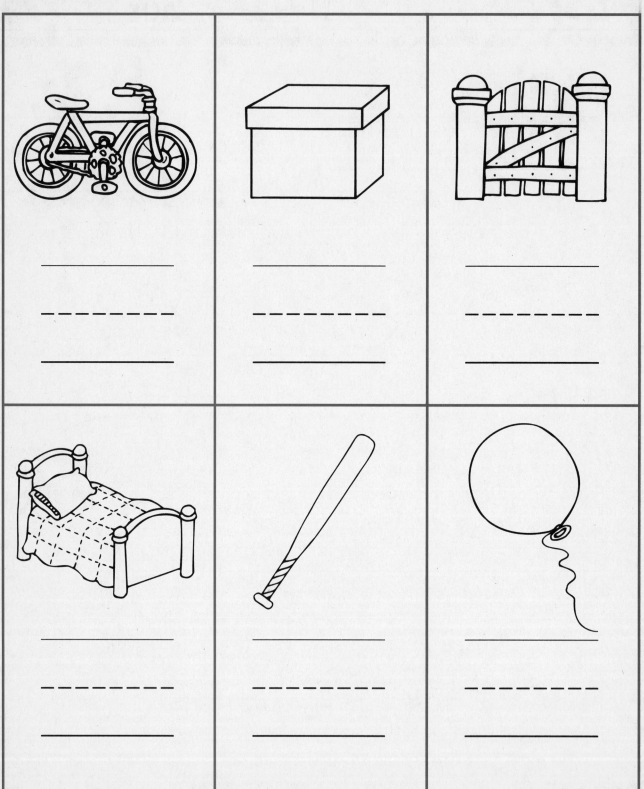

Initial b Trace and write the letters. Write *b* below each picture whose name begins with the *b* sound.

T t

tire

Name _____

Initial t   Trace and write the letters. Color the pictures whose names begin with the *t* sound.

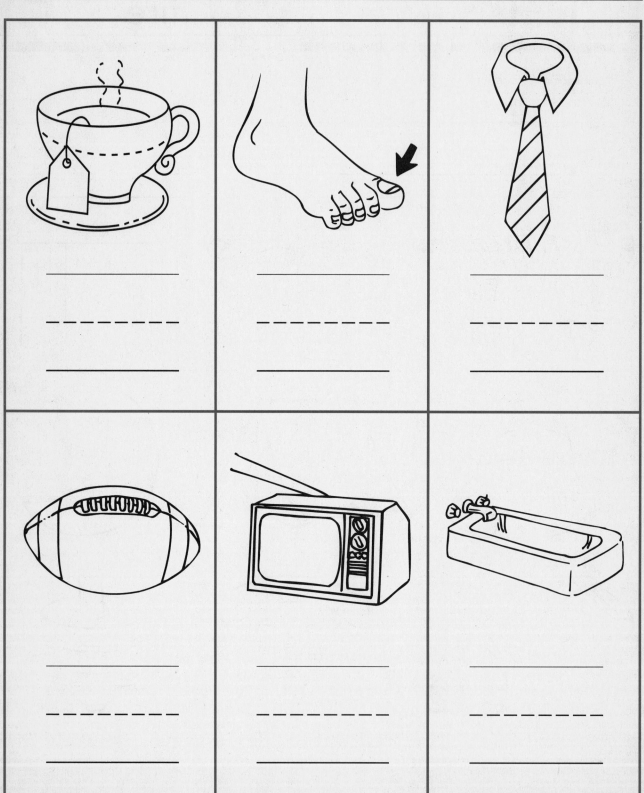

Initial t Trace and write the letters. Write *t* below each picture whose name begins with the *t* sound.

g		g		g	
b		b		b	
t		t		t	

g		g		g	
b		b		b	
t		t		t	

g		g		g	
b		b		b	
t		t		t	

Name _____

Reviewing Initial g, b, t Circle the letter that stands for the first sound in each picture name.

18 **Reviewing Initial g, b, t**   Color the block that has the *g* green, the *b* blue, and the *t* red. Then color the toys beginning with those same sounds to match.

g	g	g
b	**b**	**b**
t	t	t

g	g	g
b	**b**	**b**
t	t	t

g	g	g
b	**b**	**b**
t	t	t

Name _____

Final g, b, t   Circle the letter that stands for the last sound in each picture name.

19

Final g, b, t Write the letter that stands for the last sound in each picture name.

b

d

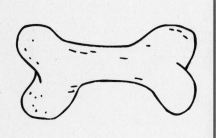  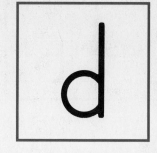

  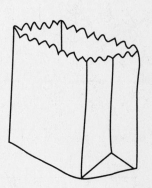

Name _____

Discriminating Initial b and d   Color the box that has the *b* blue and the *d* red. Then color the pictures beginning with those same sounds to match.

21

22 **Discriminating Final b and d** Write the letter that stands for the last sound in each picture name.

d

g

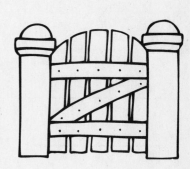

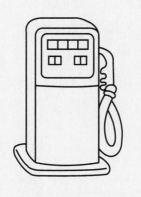

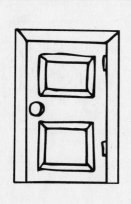

Name _____

Discriminating Initial d and g   Color the box that has the *d* brown and the *g* green. Then color the pictures beginning with those same sounds to match.

23

d		g

_ _ _ _ _ _ _ _

_____

_ _ _ _ _ _ _ _

_____

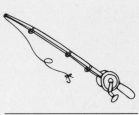

_ _ _ _ _ _ _ _

_____

_ _ _ _ _ _ _ _

_____

_ _ _ _ _ _ _ _

_____

_ _ _ _ _ _ _ _

_____

_ _ _ _ _ _ _ _

_____

24   **Discriminating Final d and g**   Write the letter that stands for the last sound in each picture name.

g	m	f
b	d	m
t	f	g

m	f	b
d	b	m
t	g	f

g	t	b
t	g	t
f	b	m

Reviewing Initial m, d, f, g, b, t   Circle the letter that stands for the first sound in each picture name.

25

© 1991 Steck-Vaughn Company

m d f g b t

_____

_____

_____

_____

_____

_____

_____

_____

© 1991 Steck-Vaughn Company

26   **Reviewing Initial m, d, f, g, b, t**   Write the letter that stands for the first sound in each picture name.

m		g		t
	d		b	m
	f		t		g

f		f		t
t		m		m
	b		d		f

g		f		b
f		g		d
	b		m		f

Name _____

Reviewing Final m, d, f, g, b, t   Circle the letter that stands for the last sound in each picture name.

© 1991 Steck-Vaughn Company

m d f g b t

Reviewing Final m, d, f, g, b, t Write the letter that stands for the last sound in each picture name.

Name _____

Initial and Final m, d, f, g, b, t   Color the picture whose name begins with the sound of the letter on the left and ends with the sound of the letter on the right.

29

m d f g b t

_ _ _ _ _ _ _ _ _ _

_____ _____

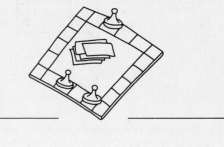

_ _ _ _ _ _ _ _ _ _

_____ _____

_ _ _ _ _ _ _ _ _ _

_____ _____

_ _ _ _ _ _ _ _ _ _

_____ _____

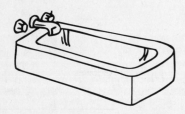

_ _ _ _ _ _ _ _ _ _

_____ _____

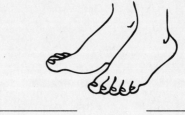

_ _ _ _ _ _ _ _ _ _

_____ _____

Initial and Final m, d, f, g, b, t Write the letters that stand for the first and last sound in each picture name.

S s

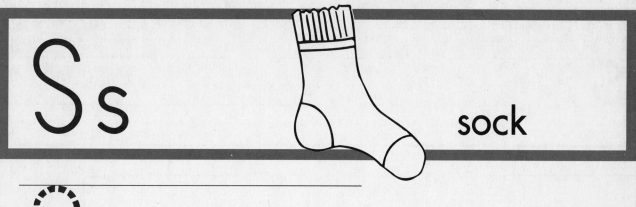

sock

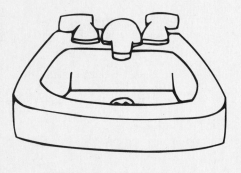

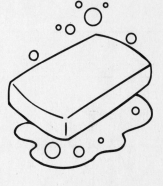

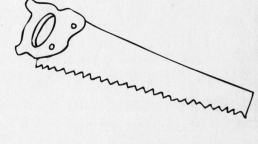

Name _____

Initial s Trace and write the letters. Color the pictures whose names begin with the *s* sound.

S s

Initial s Trace and write the letters. Write *s* below each picture whose name begins with the *s* sound.

W w

watch

Name _____

Initial w Trace and write the letters. Color the pictures whose names begin with the *w* sound.

W w

Initial w   Trace and write the letters. Write *w* below each picture whose name begins with the *w* sound.

K k

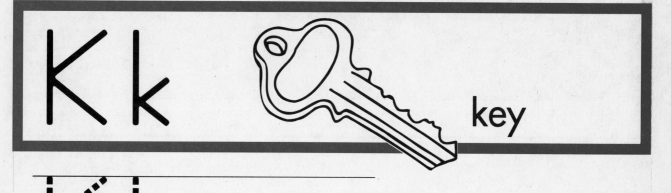

key

K k

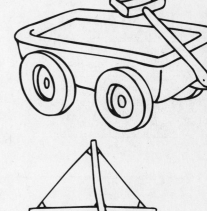

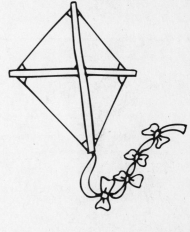

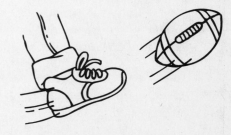

Name _____

Initial k   Trace and write the letters. Color the pictures whose names begin with the *k* sound.

k k

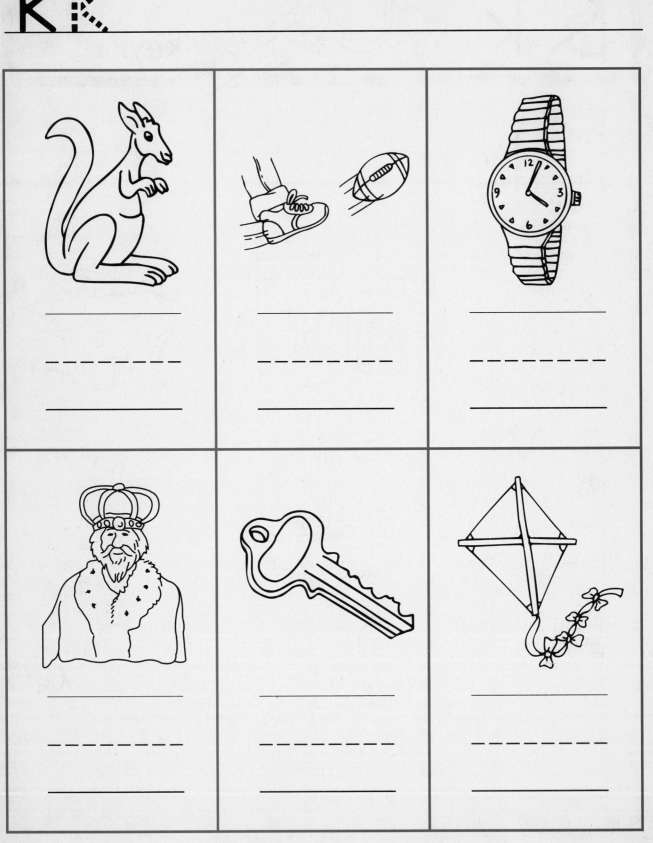

36   **Initial k**   Trace and write the letters. Write *k* below each picture whose name begins with the *k* sound.

J j

jeep

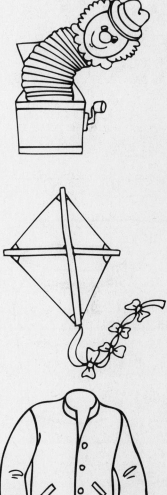

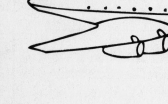

Name _____

Initial j Trace and write the letters. Color the pictures whose names begin with the *j* sound.

j J

Initial j Trace and write the letters. Write *j* below each picture whose name begins with the *j* sound.

s w k j

Name _____

Reviewing Initial s, w, k, j   Write the letter that stands for the first sound in each picture name.

Reviewing Initial s, w, k, j Color the box that has the *s* yellow, the *w* brown, the *k* orange, and the *j* red. Then color the pictures beginning with those same sounds to match.

s

k

s

k

s

k

s

k

s

k

s

k

s

k

s

k

s

k

Name _____

Final s and k   Circle the letter that stands for the last sound in each picture name.

41

Final s and k Write the letter that stands for the last sound in each picture name.

© 1991 Steck-Vaughn Company

b	s	g
w	f **7**	d
m	t	j

k	b	t
s	j	f
m	k	d

w	b	m
s	g	d
k	f	j

Name _____

Reviewing Initial Sounds   Circle the letter that stands for the first sound in each picture name.

m d f g b t w k

Reviewing Initial Sounds Write the letter that stands for the first sound in each picture name.

m		t		g
d		s		s
f		k		b

g		d		t
d		m		k
f		t		s

k		f		s
b		d		t
g		m		d

© 1991 Steck-Vaughn Company

Name _____

Reviewing Final Sounds Circle the letter that stands for the last sound in each picture name.

45

m d f g b t s k

Reviewing Final Sounds Write the letter that stands for the last sound in each picture name.

f		t
b		k
j		g
d		m

Name _____

Reviewing Initial and Final Sounds   Color the picture whose name begins with the sound of the letter on the left and ends with the sound of the letter on the right.

m d f g b t s w k j

Reviewing Initial and Final Sounds   Write the letters that stand for the first and last sound in each picture name.